One Only

Awaken to THE Relationship

By Cher Hayes

One Only
Awaken to THE Relationship

©2020 by Cher Hayes

Acknowledgements

Deepest gratitude for the Source of all creation, and all that is created. A special thanks for Lisa Nakano and family, Sharada Sheppard, Ju Ju Pang, Sabrina Stevens, and all others who supported and believed in my vision. Love, gratitude and appreciation for my three children, Tanden, Jyotin, and Trew, for being my most valuable teachers in this life and beyond.

A big THANK YOU for Viki Winterton at Expert Insights Publishing for offering her outstanding service and assisting in the entire process of connecting this book with the world.

And Thank each one of you looking at these words in this moment for Being YOU!

Introduction

This book is the language of light. It has been waiting for the right time to be assimilated and expressed, and the time is now.

Its purpose is to remind you of the one only relationship that exists: Source with Source through all the infinite expressions of creation. You are an expression/creation of Source.

This book is a handbook, intended for use as a reference and remembrance of what and why you are. In the book, you are given some of the most powerful tools and techniques to assist in clearing, transforming, and releasing the limiting energies, emotions, ideas, concepts, and beliefs (data) that are keeping you from being the fully empowered, pure expression of Source that you are.

Before reading from beginning to end, take the book in your hands, close your eyes, and ask the book what message it has for you in this moment. Consciously connect your energy with the energy of the book, and when it feels right, open it to a page as you are inspired to do so. Read that page, and most likely you will be amazed by the accuracy of your current situation and the pertinence of the message on that particular page.

You are right where you are meant to be in this exact moment. Everything you have ever experienced has brought you in the here and now. You are an important and valuable aspect of the entirety of creation. Welcome, and thank you for being you!

Table of Contents

Chapter 1:
Everything Is Energy (Light)

**"Matter is energy, energy is light,
we are all light beings."
— Albert Einstein**

I constantly remind myself of this quote in order to avoid getting lost in the physicality and fear-based drama of the human experience. I find that, if I keep my perception tuned to the light, life is much brighter!

Your body and perceived physical reality are made up of atoms, which are 99.99% energy/light. Your physical body is really an electromagnetic field of vibrating energy waves composed of photons. You are a dynamic, intelligent, vibrating, electromagnetic information field of consciousness, constantly sending and receiving information while creating and recreating the self, in relationship with the infinite expression of Source.

Physicists now validate what mystics have said for centuries: all of creation is a sea of conscious energy (light). We are droplets within/as the sea, interacting, exchanging, experiencing, and in relationship with it all.

Scientists call this energy a "field." This field has also been called *the force*, *mana*, *chi*, *prana*, and *spirit*. I often call it life. It is the universal energy field of consciousness, born from Source, which is everything and nothing. It is the Zero Point. It is the *I am*. You are the universal energy field; you are the source experiencing itself.

Source birthed all the infinite – and I mean infinite – expressions of self in order to experience itself in all possible ways. We, as instances of those expressions, are experiencing ourselves through the reflection of all that exists in the universe and the perceived physical world.

When peak states of consciousness are experienced, this is often described as being one with that field – remembering what we are. Enlightenment occurs when one realizes/remembers that *everything* is a unified field of light. It is the same when one reaches self-realization, ultimately realizing there is only *one* self, in relationship with itself, through all the different expressions of self. There is *only one relationship* being experienced in the universe – Source – with Source as *you* and *all* of creation.

It's time to wake up and remember what and why we are! It is time to recognize ourselves as everything that exists. Realize that you are Source experiencing itself as you! See, feel, remember, and experience yourself as the universal energy field of consciousness. You, everyone, and everything *is*. See it all around you. See it in nature, in all beings, all that exists. Recognize *yourself* as a reflection of all that you perceive. Remember *you* as Source. Look at anyone or anything throughout the day and say to yourself, *I am that*. Start to recognize the energy and similarity of all beings. Realize that not only are we the same Source essence, but we also share the same molecules that come from the stars of our Universe that manifests as the .00001% physical substance of our body.

This is the most wonderful time in human existence. We have all been given the opportunity and are being invited by the highest aspect of our self (Source) to awaken to the reality of what and why we are. It is happening now – I see it all over the world. There are big changes going on in the evolution of human consciousness. This is the time of remembering, experiencing, perceiving, integrating, and embodying the fully empowered, highest vibration of self. This is remembering there is only one self that is in relationship with itself, through all of the infinite expressions of self.

I will share with you a very powerful meditation and a oneness integration practice for you to apply in order to truly get understand this concept so that you can embody it and know it with all of your being. I highly recommend you do the meditation at least 10 minutes when you wake up in the morning and perform the oneness integration practice throughout the day.

<u>Meditation</u>: Sit or lie down in a quiet place where you will not be disturbed. Bring all of your awareness/attention into your body, focusing on your breath going in and out. Bring the awareness of your breath to your toes and slowly go up your legs, through your torso, up your fingertips, through your arms, up your neck, and through the top of your head. Imagine and feel every cell, molecule, and strand of DNA awakening and vibrating as the life force energy of pure consciousness. Consciously connect and ask the empowering energy/light of Source to purify every cell and activate your DNA to the highest potential possible in this moment. Feel each cell emitting and receiving the light energy of Source. Feel the energy vibrating as your **real** body – your electromagnetic field of light. Focus on your heart area and give love and gratitude to yourself for doing

this work. Recognize yourself as the energy and expression of Source.

Allow your entire being to immerse in this vibration until it is fully embodied. Imagine the presence of Source as your essence; feel it with all your being until you *know* it as *you*. Ultimately you will see all perceived "others" and everything that exists as an energy field with a particular frequency signature within the one field of consciousness.

<u>Oneness Integration Practice</u>: Apply this throughout the day. While you are driving, bored at work, washing dishes, in the elevator, in line at the store, walking down the street, etc., remind yourself of the vibrational feeling you get with the meditation above. Bring that feeling into every cell of your body. Feel your energy body and physical body vibrating as one. Feel the energy body expand out of the parameters of your physical body, creating a large bubble around you. Be aware of the feeling of your energy body expanding more and more with each breath. Focus on your heart area and add the feeling of love and gratitude for yourself and all that exists. As you are aware of this feeling, watch your bubble continue to expand across the entire planet and through the universe, through all dimensions, unified with the infinite creation of Source.

Here's a fun experiment to try as you're expanding your bubble of energy: if others are around, focus on the energy going towards one person and watch for a possible reaction. They might turn your direction or even come up to you to talk. Or maybe a smile will come to their face.

You will also notice that the more you practice raising the vibration of your energy field, the more magnetized you will become, causing people and things to just gravitate towards you. It is a really powerful manifestation tool.

I can guarantee that, if you engage in both of these practices daily, not only will every aspect of your life change for the better quite quickly, but you will also start to experience synchronicities and miracles more and more in your life. And if you give a deep sense of gratitude to life for these experiences the moment you get them, then life will keep giving you more.

Chapter 2:
Frequency and Vibration

"If you want to find the secrets of the universe, think in terms of energy, frequency, and vibration."
— Nikola Tesla

The perceived physical domain consists of various frequencies of energy waves vibrating slowly enough to be observed by the physical eye as light. This causes the concept of the physical to appear real.

All is experienced through a spectrum of light that is vibrating at different frequencies. Everything that exists, including you, is made up of vibrating energy waves within the field of consciousness. The only difference between you and anything or anyone else is your particular frequency signature. Your frequency vibrates as a field of electromagnetic energy, communicating and exchanging information in relationship with all that exists within the universal energy field of consciousness.

What constitutes a particular frequency signature is the quality of consciousness and state of mind, resulting from thought, emotion, perception, belief, action, and experience. Our perception of experience is filtered through the data in the subconscious mind that we have accumulated since conception. It is absolutely impossible for two people to have the exact same perception of an experience in a given moment. Each of us is living in our own world, built upon on our individual life experiences and perceptions of those experiences. We are unique, individual expressions of consciousness within the collective consciousness of humanity as an expression/experience of Source.

Human consciousness is expressed through a frequency spectrum of emotion. The lowest end is contracted, suppressed energy expressed as shame, guilt, apathy, grief, anger, or fear – all suffering. The middle comprises pride, courage, willingness, acceptance, and reason – all used for just getting by. The more energetically expanded, higher and highest frequency emotions are love, gratitude, peace, compassion, joy, ecstasy, bliss, and enlightenment. These all embody oneness Every human has the potential to experience the entire spectrum; we *are* the entire spectrum. It is your quality of consciousness and state of mind that determines what frequency you experience. Most move in and out of different frequencies throughout their lives, and even throughout the day. We are all experiencing the same human reality, just at slightly different vibratory degrees.

A high-vibe person's thoughts and emotions are expressed with creativity, fun, gratitude, awe, excitement, acceptance, connection, and joy; these are *love*-based emotions. Such people are usually physically active, self-motivated, healthy, energy givers, and people love being around them (as they are full of energy, light, and life). A low-vibe person's thoughts and emotions are expressed as anger, worry, guilt, resentment, hate, jealousy, boredom, separation; these are *fear*-based emotions. Such people are usually physically lazy, unmotivated, unhealthy energy vampires, and people usually don't feel good around them unless they are of a similar vibe (depleted of energy, light, and life).

We attract and magnetize our vibrational-frequency match. Like forces attract; it's a classic rule of physics. We are magnets. We are electromagnetic beings who magnetize into our lives exactly what we are communicating to the universe with our thoughts, emotions, and vibration. Whatever thought frequency we are transmitting must come back to us due to the laws of physics, especially if there is emotion (magnetically charged vibrational waves) attached to the thought. So whether it's high-vibrational joy or low-vibrational worry, that which we vibrationally communicate in any moment is what we're attracting back, personally experiencing, and contributing to the experience we are all collectively sharing.

Depending upon a frequency's vibration, it has the ability to heal or harm you. Scientists use technology to determine the frequency levels of the human body. A normal human body's frequency is between 62-78 MHz. They found that if you keep your body's frequency rate at above 60 MHz, you are less prone to sickness. Thoughts, emotions, environment, food, music, and electromagnetic energies from cell phones, computers, and electronic devices, all affect your body's frequency and well-being.

If you are unsure about the effects your environment has on your well-being, try residing for a few days in a place inhabited by low-vibe people, and then try one with high-vibe people. Or a toxic environment with chemicals, trash, and noise, vs. a place that is nontoxic, clean, and quiet. For many doing this, the effects will be immediate, and for others, it could take a bit more time to really feel the difference.

Most people have heard the saying, "You are what you eat." Based on my experience, this is true. I challenge you to eat only high-vibe, raw foods (fruits, vegetables, nuts and seeds, sprouted grains, legumes, raw nut butters, healthy oils like olive and coconut, super-food shakes, fermented foods, seaweed, and sprouts) for 30 days or more and find out for yourself.

Music is a tough one for me to address, because my personal thought is that whatever moves you is what's beneficial for you. However, I would like to bring to mind the reality of the impact different musical frequencies have on your overall state of being. Ancient tuning practices used the Just Intonation Chart, producing the Solfeggio frequencies, which were much purer in sound than our modern-day musical scale. The Solfeggio frequencies were used in sacred music like the Gregorian Chants. The Solfeggio tones comprise frequencies meant to balance your energy and keep your body, mind, and spirit in perfect harmony. Around the 16th century, Western cultures adopted the Twelve-Tone Equal Temperament, which mistunes all consonant intervals except the octave.

Many believe this change was done purposely by the rulers of the time to keep the populace out of tune and harmony with their natural, healthy, creative, empowered state and cause suppression of emotions, lack of consciousness, and submissiveness, ultimately leading to mental and physical disease. You can listen to very powerful, healing, and transformative music with the different Solfeggio tones on YouTube. There are also many other types of beneficial music for the body, mind, and spirit. After listening to them, you will naturally relax into the tones.

There was a profound experiment done by Dr. Masaru Emoto on the effects of what different music does to water. He would freeze and take photographs of water after playing different music and saying different words or prayers to the water. Again and again, his experiments showed that classical music produced beautiful, coherent crystals shapes, and heavy-metal music produced misshapen, incoherent crystals. He also found that saying positive words like "gratitude," and "love" produced beautiful, perfect crystals, and negative words like "hate" or "kill" produced ill-shaped crystals. Since our bodies are 70% water, you can imagine what negative thoughts, emotions, and words do to yourself, those around you, and the unified collective consciousness of humanity.

Chapter 3:
Electromagnetism

"We physically are little units of electrical energy, and we vibrate and project electromagnetic thought."
– John Trudell

Every organ, muscle, and cell of the body has its own electromagnetic energy field, which is what generates your overall electromagnetic energy field. Scientists call this field that your body emanates a biofield. Because the body's circuitry is electric, it creates a magnetic energy field around it.

The heart's electrical field is about 60 times greater in amplitude than the electrical activity generated by the brain. The heart is the greatest electrical generator of the body and the energetic biofield. Due to the continuous pumping, it creates a magnetic field around itself that permeates your energetic biofield. Because the blood is a good conductor of electricity, the entire circulatory system pulses with electricity each time the heart beats. The heart creates electrical, heat, light, pressure, sound, and magnetic and electromagnetic signals. The heart-field creates a synchronizing communication signal to every cell in the body in a manner similar to information carried by radio waves. The heart-rate variability is distinctly altered by different emotions, which is felt by every cell. This energy is not only transmitted internally but is also detectable by others within its range of communication. Just as the organs and cells of our body are in relationship with each other, each with its own role and in constant communication, working together to keep the body in balance, we too are a cell in the body of the universe, in relationship with each other, living our role, working together, affecting each other, and in constant communication with each other and the entire universe through our thoughts, emotions, and vibration – the biofield.

The function of a neuron is to receive information from other neurons, to process that information, and then send the information to other neurons. Neurons process all of the information that flows in and out of the central nervous system. They process the information through which we are able to reason, think, dream, plan, and remember all we do with our minds and all we do with our senses, like seeing, hearing, smelling, tasting, touching, and moving our bodies. There are an estimated 10,000 types of neurons and 100 billion neurons in the brain alone. Just as the neurons are information processors and are in relationship to and in constant communication with the physical body, we too are in relationship to and in constant communication, exchanging information, and affecting all that exists in the universe through the vibrational frequency of our thoughts and feelings. We are the neurons of our planet.

All of existence is the creation of Source experiencing and interacting with itself. Everything is in a constant flux of giving, exchanging, in relationship with, and interacting as Energy. Each individual energy field has an influence on the world, and vice versa. We are all connected energetically and are in the most intimate relationship with each other and the entire universe, within and as one single field of existence. Through the vibration of our individual field, we affect everything and everyone in the body of our planet and the entire universe.

Our bodies are bombarded 24 hours a day by artificial, electromagnetic fields (EMFs), causing various and dangerous health problems. Studies have shown a link between exposure to artificial EMF and an increased rate of brain tumors, leukemia, various forms of cancer, and numerous other health problems. These dangerous artificial EMFs are coming from circuit-breakers (very toxic), air conditioners, microwave ovens, in-floor electrical heating, fluorescent lighting, halogen ceiling lights, electric sockets, computers, cordless phones, landline phones, hairdryers, etc. – basically everything that uses artificial electricity.

The artificial EMFs disrupt the integrity and coherence of the intricate communication of the mind-body system, leading to malfunction and mental confusion. If the body is completely out of balance, they can cause death. Generations that are still amongst us were not assailed by the overload of the artificial EMFs we have today. I have not met one person who does not know someone or have a family member who has or had cancer, and the way things are going, with 5G and all the new technologies being created, I think we would benefit as a species if we did our best to protect ourselves and do what we can to keep our biological system functioning optimally.

One of the best ways I know to continuously revamp and detoxify your entire system is through grounding. Artificial EMFs are positively charged and have a negative affect on the body in various ways. Our Earth's natural surface is negatively charged and has a rebalancing, reorganizing, cleansing, and detoxing effect on our bodies' bioenergetic system. All you have to do is put your bare feet on the ground (best if raw earth) and recharge in the negatively charged electrons.

Going into nature amongst the trees, rocks, sand, and water is immensely beneficial to your overall well-being. If you are not able to get your bare feet onto the earth or go out into nature, there are also devices you can get to re-stabilize your system. You can also purchase a protective case and covering for your cell phone and computer. Avoid body contact with your phone and computer as much as possible, and do your best not to have it in your pocket or on your lap. It is highly suggested that you not sleep with your computer or phone on or near you.

While we cannot easily eliminate artificial EMFs from our environment completely, we can do our best to reduce our exposure to them.

Chapter 4:
Consciousness

**"Consciousness is the field of all possibilities...
that subsequently manifest as space-time
events. And I am the field."
— Deepak Chopra**

Everything in the universe is a mode of consciousness, being experienced in infinite formations. Within the collective consciousness, we lost conscious connection to the essence of what we are – formless, unconditioned consciousness. Our true selves became clothed in a conditioned physical self from genetics, the environment we were raised, and all the data from experience we've downloaded into our sub-conscious mind from all of our interactions and experience.

The time is *now* for a radical upgrade in human consciousness; we must awaken and remember our true selfves as Source experiencing the universe. It is already happening; the entire universe is evolving extraordinarily right now, releasing higher vibrational frequencies directly from Source. Since you are the universe, you are already going through this. You can choose to consciously participate and enjoy this rapid change by aligning with the frequencies and allowing them to integrate, stabilize, and be embodied. The ultimate way to do this is with 100% acceptance of what is and total surrender to the Source plan. We must also contribute to the process by taking full responsibility for all that we experience within and without.

We each have a responsibility to help clear and transmute the false limiting beliefs, concepts, and thoughts within our portion of oneself. It's the main reason we are having this experience on Earth in this timeline. If each one of us takes 100% responsibility for what we are experiencing in our reality and we choose to do the inner work, then as a collective, we will completely change our reality to the ideal and align with the Source plan; we will experience consciously *being Source* experiencing the universe. We will acknowledge ourselves and all other selves as Source, experiencing life in physical form on this awesome planet. This is our destiny; this is why we are here. This is the plan from Source. No more blaming anything on the outside for our unhappiness or misfortune. Each one of us has to do our part to clean up the inside so that the outside will correspond accordingly. Let go of the past regarding who gave you this pain or unbearable experience. It's done.

The past is done! It gave you the strength, compassion, understanding, and all of the characteristics that you have now to be able to do the work which needs to be done – to play out your role as it was meant to be. See the gift in each experience, then thank it, love it, and let it go! Choose to live in the present moment and clear and transmute all that is not in resonance with the ideal highest aspect of you, the one who knows it is **one** with the universe - the one that remembers, *I am* Source, the one who wants to be free.

You are already are enlightened; you are a magnificent field of light! You are all the power and intelligence of the universe. You are Source experiencing the universe. What is being asked of all humans in this timeline which we are collectively experiencing is to wake up from the amnesia of the collective consciousness and remember what and why we are. Let us realize we are one self and imagine and align with our ideal dream, the Source plan, together.

The way this is done is by each one of us taking full responsibility of our experiences. Take ownership of your thoughts, feelings, actions, and reality you are experiencing. Everything you experience in this perceived physical dimension is through your mind/body system. Your experience is filtered through all the sub-conscious data you collected since conception. You were born as pure awareness, taking in sensually everything around you. You were still connected to the senses of awareness beyond the physical and were still consciously connected to your relationship with universal consciousness and all that exists. You were in awe of this reality until you started to be taught the limiting concepts, labels, and beliefs of what reality is within the societal collective unconsciousness.

You adopted your conditioned egoic self of limiting data, like we all have, and it is the responsibility of each one of us to clear and transmute all of the false data collected within our own sub-consciousness realm and ultimately the entire collective unconsciousness.

I know it seems like a huge task, but remember that we have each other. Once you make the decision to contribute your part to do the inner work, life is guaranteed to give you all of the assistance necessary for your particular needs. We are in this together. You are not alone. We are all *one*.

I have spent 39 years now traveling the world meeting healers and spiritual teachers, attending hundreds of seminars, completing internships, reading thousands of books, and clearing clients, all while looking for the newest and best way to help myself and others clear and transmute the limiting false ideas, concepts, beliefs, traumas, and energies that we have acquired in our lives within the collective consciousness of humanity. My life mission has been to help free humanity from these blocks so that we can *unite* consciously as our true selves, the one self, Source, *I am*.

I will share with you the most powerful process that the majority of therapist, healers, and other explorers of consciousness and I use in our repertoire. I will also share an extremely powerful one from my beloved Hawaiian Islands. I have used both since my mid-20s and continue to do so today when needed.

If any of you think your situation is too much to deal with, think of this: I have always said the reason I'm such a good Transformation Facilitator is because I have personally gone through almost all of the major human challenges in life. And the challenges I didn't personally go through, I have helped clear clients who have. All of those experiences helped me to relate, understand, and have compassion for my clients and all people in general. I had to do a lot of work on myself to process the traumas, blocked energies, false beliefs, and fears I acquired from those experiences, but it also gave me the tools to help others. At first, I believed there was an ending to the personal inner work. There were times I thought I was free from emotional triggers and reactions. Then life gave me someone or something to push me even deeper. So I accepted the inner work process as a way of life and actually started to welcome and enjoy watching a new one arise. Later I learned that, when you reach the place at which you may have worked all of your "personal stuff," you realize that there's no such thing as personal stuff. We are **all one**, so the stuff keeps coming until we all finish the work together.

This first process is truly extremely powerful. It is drawn from "The Work," by Byron Katie. You will use four questions to inquire within yourself, using the questions as a meditation, finding the deepest meaning to the answers that only *you* can reveal. You will realize that you already have all the answers to any problem or question you may have. Then you can do the turnaround to examine the issue from another angle. If you use this process as a constant tool for transformation whenever you are upset about anything, you will in each usage become freer and freer of the limiting ideas, concepts, and beliefs that are preventing you from realizing your true self – your one only self.

One of the most well-known gurus of India, Ramana Maharshi, has visitors from thousands of people from all over the world who come for spiritual answers. He most frequently comments to them,

"There are only two reliable methods for attaining self-realization: one could either pursue self-inquiry or one could surrender." I totally agree with this statement, and that is why "The Work" is so powerful: it is all about self-inquiry.

I will give you here an example of how to use, "The Work," from a video Byron Katie posted on YouTube. You can also download the worksheet for free at thework.com

First focus on who or what upsets you. For example, a woman feels upset because she claims, "My husband doesn't care about me." She will take this belief and ask herself these four questions:

1.Is it true?
2.Can you absolutely know that it is true? (Meditate on this, go deep within, beyond your conscious ego mind. Notice what comes up.)
3.How do you react when you believe that thought? (Notice all your feelings about that thought. Notice all the images past, present, and future when you think that thought.)
4.Who would you be without that thought? Imagine yourself without the thought. How would you be around your husband without that thought?

Through this exercise, you will realize that your thoughts about anything are the cause of all suffering. Without your thought about it, you cannot suffer. It is our belief about what is happening, not what is actually happening, that causes our distress.

Next, consider the opposite:

1. Change "He doesn't care about me" to "He does care about me" (go deep within this thought. Remember "The Work" is used as a meditation).
2. Another opposite is this: "I don't care about him" (find genuine examples to when you have been uncaring towards him). You can use this time to apologize within yourself or also to him in person. Make amends; make it right within yourself and him if that is what it requires to make it right within yourself.
3. Another turnaround is this: "I don't care about me" (get very still with this and discover genuine examples of how you have not cared about yourself).

Most often, after doing this process, the emotional charge will have dissipated, and you may even find amusement in it. "The Work" is meditation and contemplation. It takes very deep stillness.

This next one is an extremely potent ancient Hawaiian healing method called Ho'oponopno. Ihaleakala Hew Len, Ph.D, is one of the most prominent practitioners of Ho'oponopno. His story of his miraculous transformation of the environment in a chaotic mental hospital without even coming into contact with the staff has inspired me and others all over the world. Based on the fact that you are your world and everything you experience is a reflection of you, he took 100% responsibility for all of the patients and staff at this institution. He took their records and staff information, and one by one, he worked on himself (not them) using Ho'oponopno, with the consciousness that the reason they are in his reality is because he had an aspect (similar data) of their issue within him. Using this process only and never coming into contact with the patients, within time, the violence was gone, the staff became more balanced, and the entire atmosphere of the hospital changed for the better of all.

Ho'oponopono Clearing and Self-Identity Practice uses four powerful phrases:
1. "I am sorry" (you can say this without specifying for what)
2. "Please forgive me" (you are making amends for data that needs to be corrected)
3. "Thank you" (you don't need to specify for what)

4. "I love you" (the infinite power of love)

You can use these phrases to clear a specific problem for yourself, and you can use it on yourself for others (knowing they are a reflection of you). You do not use it to heal others by directing it at them. It has to be used through you, taking responsibility as them, being your reflection. Say these phrases within while connecting to the highest aspect of you/Source. This is a way of connecting and communicating your conscious self with your subconscious self and your superconscious self to do the clearing together with Source. Ho'oponopono means to correct an error using repentance, forgiveness, and transmutation. This involves ultimately clearing all data you've collected in your subconscious mind, becoming *free* of the collective conscious data, thus allowing you to remember what you are: your true identity as Source.

Chapter 5.
Mind, Thought, and Power

**"When you become the master of your mind,
you are master of everything."
—Swami Satchidananda**

All matter you perceive in the physical world is manifested from the mind using thought to align with the already-created universe within the infinite energy field of consciousness. Modern physicists successfully proved through the double-slit experiment that the observer shapes reality. This experiment shows that light and matter display characteristics of both waves and particles; it starts out as a wave, and once it is observed, it turns into a particle. We manifest matter with the observation of the mind.

The human experience of mind is a process of consciousness to have an objective experience through the human mind/body system. There are four fundamental aspects of the human mind: conscious, sub-conscious, collective conscious, and superconscious. The conscious mind identifies, compares, and analyzes the incoming information from the senses, decides to accept or reject the data, then immediately is encoded in the subconscious mind. The subconscious mind not only controls the function of your body's temperature, heart rate, breathing, and functional homeostasis, but it also retrieves and stores *all* of the experiential data that the conscious mind accepts. It then reflects back to the conscious mind the memories, beliefs, ideas, and concepts you have consciously accepted of yourself and the world to ensure that you "stick to the program," and stay safe. 95% of our behaviors and reactions happen at the subconscious level. These run on auto-pilot, and the main function of the subconscious is to conserve brain energy, abide by the data the conscious mind accepted, and keep you alive. Next is the collective conscious mind, which not only is where all of your thoughts and emotions are encoded, but is *one* with all the thoughts and emotions of humanity. Then there is the superconscious mind, which is the highest vibrational field of mind. This is the cosmic mind, the infinite/Source mind, where *all* thoughts, emotions, and experiences of all of existence is recorded. This dimension of mind is called by many the Akashic Records. When you clean and clear the false limiting data in the subconscious mind, free yourself from the collective consciousness, become the master of your conscious mind, and unite your conscious and subconscious mind with the superconscious, you align the seven dimensional frequencies of your Chakras (vortexes of energy), allowing you to tune in and become *one* with the mind of source.

The power of the mind is limitless. In the ancient Hermetic teachings, the number one principle of the seven principles for self-mastery is "The Principle of Mentalism." This first principle was considered the most important and governs over the other six. The Principle of Mentalism relates to how the mind harnesses universal energy to manifest, destroy, and manipulate matter within the infinite intelligent field of consciousness. Although the Hermetic teachings date back to the 1st century A.D., they are most well known for their influence during the 15th century and the Renaissance. They resurfaced again with the Freemasons and were also in the teachings of the American revolutionaries. The leaders and great thinkers of the world know and utilize the power of the mind. The charisma of the world's powerful and influential people comes from the energetic vibrational frequency of their mind. It is even more powerful if it is coupled with the power of emotion (both fear and love based) and the most powerful if that person's mind is in tune with the mind of Source.

The mind, brain, and body work together as a collective thought-wave transmitter and receiver. Like vibrations of light and sound, thought vibrations radiate out in all directions. We are constantly communicating by sending and receiving information with thought waves to and from the universal energy field of consciousness. The frequency of your mind/body that is generated from your thoughts and emotions tunes you into the resonant frequency within the infinite electromagnetic spectrum of energy and information. This is just like when you tune into a different radio station to listen to the specific frequency of sound and information.

A good example of this is when different people from all over the world will come up with the idea to invent, write, or create the exact same thing without ever coming into contact with each other. This is how similar pyramid structures and the same sacred images were used in different places on the planet before their creators could have ever come into contact with one another. On a personal note, there have been at least 8 books of information I was tuned into since my early 20s that I didn't end up writing, but someone else did. Inspirational ideas are lingering in the atmosphere, and if you are tuned into the same wavelength (information field), it will be the same message, though filtered through your own particular brainwave coding from the data in your subconscious mind.

The mind uses thought to invent, experience, manifest, and destroy. *Everything* we use and experience started with a thought: clothes, shampoo, furniture, homes, buildings, paintings, music, war, companies, *everything* – even who you believe yourself to be. We all created the image of ourselves, our ego, by the thoughts and beliefs we accumulated when we were young children. This image of self becomes the core of who we believe ourselves to be, which modifies as we grow older and collect more thoughts/beliefs about self. As Buddha said, "The mind is everything. What you think, you become." If you really understand the power of the mind and the usage of your thoughts, then you can choose to become a master of your mind/thoughts and create the *ideal you* and the *ideal reality* we can all share.

If you desire self-mastery, self-realization, and the freedom to be the fully empowered ideal, real you, then **the time is now**. The first and most important step is to take 100% responsibility for *all* of your thoughts, feelings, and experiences. The second step is to realize that it has to be done by inviting and integrating your conscious, subconscious, and superconscious aspects of the mind.

You can meditate to communicate this intent with your mind or speak the intent out loud with all your being, saying, "I am ready and willing to release all thought patterns that do not serve and resonate with the highest potential and the ideal expression of Source through me." The third step is to begin the diligent practice of clearing out all of the false and limiting ideas, concepts, and beliefs that are the programmed data in your subconscious mind you have collected throughout your life about yourself and your reality of the world.

In addition to using "The Work" described in chapter 4, I will outline the Bubble Technique, which you can use throughout the day. As you make these practices a way of life, you will begin to use them naturally and actually start to enjoy the process. Notice your dreams, and write them down as soon as you wake up. When you do this, you are communicating with your subconscious mind that you are consciously working with it in order to understand and release deep feelings. During this stage of working these suppressed emotions, use Ho'oponopono as each emotion comes up. You can also go deeper with the process by allowing yourself to fully feel the emotion and thank it for coming to the surface, look into your past, and find the original thought/belief within it. Then use "The Work" and transmute the energy.

When you look at other people, see yourself in them and them in you. Thank them in your heart for being a reflection of you and send them love. You will notice very quickly how people respond to you in a more positive way than before and open up on a deeper level. You don't even have to say a word to them; their subconscious and superconscious will resonate with your loving vibe. When you experience a synchronicity or if you get a message or answer to a question you had through another person, song, or what would seem some random way, thank your subconscious and superconscious mind for communicating with you. By expressing constant love, gratitude, and acceptance for all that is going on, you are fostering the most beautiful, powerful, and only relationship you can ever have: the relationship of Source with Source as you, through all the levels of mind, consciousness, and existence.

The Bubble Technique is a way of using the power of awareness to transform the false limiting ideas, concepts, and beliefs in your subconscious mind that causes 95% of your thoughts, reactions, and behaviors in the present moment. Don't underestimate the undeniable force of awareness; you will be delighted with how efficiently it works.

All throughout the day or as often as you can, bring awareness to your thoughts and words. Listen to yourself speak, and be aware of how you use your words. The power of words is sharper than any sword. As stated in the Gospel, "the word became flesh and made his dwelling among us." It is extremely important what you say after the words *I am*. Listen to yourself when you say these words. If you are saying them in any other way than "I am God" or "I am Source," "I am the universe," or "I am," then you are reducing yourself into something you are not. Pay attention to what other people are saying. Notice thoughts and words that are untrue or of a negative, limiting nature. Listen carefully to what you and others say, and ask yourself, *Is that really true? Where did that thought or idea come from? How do I know it is really true?* When you bring awareness to the negative or untrue thoughts and words, ask yourself if that thought is in resonance and a benefit to the highest vibrational aspect of self. If the answer is no, then instantly create a mental bubble and put the thought inside the bubble and say to the universe, I send this to be released and transmuted on all levels of my mind and the collective mind of all that exist, *so be it!*

Chapter 6:
Awareness

"Rather than being your thoughts and emotions, be the awareness behind them."
– Eckart Tolle

Existence is Source being aware of itself as presence energy in the potential field of consciousness vibrating the frequency of unconditional love, using light to experience form. It is through awareness that you are able to know what you are and why you exist. When you become the observer of awareness, you acknowledge the presence of Source as you. "*I am*" is infinite awareness.

Awareness can only be experienced in the **now**. It's in the stillness of mind in the present moment during which you tap into the powerful presence energy in the universal field of consciousness. This is how you awaken your mind and body to the essence of Source, which is loving awareness beyond the cognitive mind. When thinking is replaced by stillness, presence, and awareness, then you can receive the pure information and energy directly from Source.

To become aware of this presence, you still your mind and feel the energy field of your body. This energy field is your vibrational blueprint that configures your perceived physical body and is the purest expression of the droplet of you within/as the sea of your presence energy/Source. It is what you consciously connect with when you do the meditation I showed you in Chapter One. After you moved your attention from thinking to feeling, then you go beyond that to just pure awareness of all that is in the now. One mantra that I say to myself whenever I become aware that my mind has gotten caught in a thought pattern is this: *be still and feel.* I immediately bring my attention to my energy body then I expand into awareness of the presence of Source. For years, I used the very powerful command, "Be still and know I am God" during meditation, so my mind/body is used to silencing when I say *Be still.* While in a deep state of meditation, it is beneficial to program into your subconscious mind certain cues to use when you are not meditating to assist in bringing your mind into the present moment with awareness of presence, instead of thinking.

As you perform the clearing methods given in this book, you will naturally become more aware as you release the old limiting programmed story of who, what, and why you are. You will start to perceive the dimensional layers of consciousness in action and become aware of the deeper meaning of events. You will not take things personally anymore; if it bothers you, then perform "The Work," Ho'oponopono, or one of the other methods described herein to cleanse it. That's *why* you exist – to clear all the false data in human unconsciousness and allow Source the freedom to experience itself as you without any limitation. You will see the connection and bigger picture of all that is happening and become the unattached, accepting witness to Source revealing itself. As you expand your awareness, you will see clearly the similarity of other selves in other people, yet observe how beautifully unique they are at the same time. With detached awareness of self, the knowing of self broadens. You can then see yourself in all perceived others and ultimately be aware that you and all other selves are one self in relationship as Source.

"Those who are highly evolved maintain an undiscriminating perception. Seeing everything, labeling nothing, they maintain their awareness of the Great Oneness. Thus they are supported by it." – Laozi

Chapter 7: Many Me's

"Each person you meet is an aspect of yourself, clamoring for love."
– Eric Micha'el Leventhal

After implementing Byron Katie's "The Work" into my life, I came up with a shortcut version that was immediate and the catalyst to awakening the perception of myself in everyone: as soon as I notice that I'm judging another, I ask myself, *Is there a part of me that's like that?*

I started using it whenever I would have an emotional issue with someone. In the beginning, I noticed my ego rationalizing and making my similarity not as bad as the other's negative qualities. For example, my father and I always had a strained relationship, I considered him selfish, self-centered, and arrogant. When I asked myself, "is there a part of me that is like that?" my answer was, "well, maybe yes, *but not as much as him*!" I had to laugh at myself for that one. Another example is when I got upset with my boyfriend because he was being so immature. As soon as I noticed my accusation of him, I asked myself, "Is there a part of me that is immature?" And, of course, the answer was yes. It was quite obvious when I looked back at my immature reaction during the argument about him being immature! What really woke me up was when I found myself comparing a new wonderful boyfriend to the last deep, dark, difficult one, saying to myself how happy I was to "now have one that is just like me." I realized I had to accept that they are both like me.

I use this method on everyone that comes into my awareness, and I cannot find one person that isn't an aspect of me. Try it out for yourself; I guarantee that, if they are in your conscious reality, they are an aspect of you. The politician you don't like, the annoying boss, the rude neighbor, the greedy capitalist, and so on. This doesn't apply only to the ones that annoy you, it is also those you admire; gurus, brilliant inventors, change-making activist, saints, and great artists are *all* are an aspect of you. Ultimately, you become aware that they don't have to be in your conscious reality to be an aspect of you, because *all is one* in the universal-unified field of consciousness, so *all is you*.

When you come to this realization, then you know that, in judging them, you are judging yourself. The moment you start to judge another/yourself, do

Ho'oponono and cleanse all judgment out of your field. Then you will start to see that most people are trapped in the programmed data of their subconscious mind and the collective consciousness; they are all doing their best to survive, yearning to break out of the prison of warped perception and for the freedom to express as the magnificent being that they are. Then judgment is transformed into compassion, and you start to experience more of the energy/light/love of yourself and all other selves.

This is *why* you are experiencing life on Earth. This is the plan designed by Source/you. This is the timeline for each one of us to wake up from the amnesia of collective consciousness, to break free from the confinement of all mental limitations, and realize or remember what we are as a unique expression of Source.

Chapter 8.
Trust Issues

**"The fault, dear Brutus, is not in our stars, but in ourselves."
— William Shakespeare**

Children learn to lie to their guardians, teachers, and religious leaders to avoid punishment and to their friends and others to fit in. Most people created a persona that is fake in order to get along in society.

We experience lies everywhere – in our religions, politics, social media, advertising, work place, friends, partnerships, and all variations of relationships. Consciously, most have become numb to the web of lies we all share. We have collectively created a reality of deception, within and without, continuously feeding it each time we choose to tell that "little white lie." We rationalize it, saying we don't want to hurt another by being sincere. But in truth, you are not only hurting the other more by lying, you are also hurting yourself and your ability to trust yourself.

We are taught to behave, be polite, and say the right things. The majority acquire a skill of saying what they think the other wants them to say instead of what they are really thinking or feeling. Although it's thoughtful to refrain from saying things that may be hurtful or offensive to another's personality, it's harmful to both self and other self to outright lie. I shared this topic with a friend before writing this chapter, and I know I probably shouldn't have been shocked by her response, knowing she is traditional in societal ways. However, I was still surprised when she said "You are supposed to be one way out in public, and your real self at home." Wow! If this is the socially excepted norm, it makes one wonder if this has anything to do with the overwhelming numbers of people diagnosed with bi-polar disorder. Do the people who feel isolated and like they don't fit in do so because they are not able to master the social requirement of creating a false self? Even worse is the case of those who feel like they are a total failure in life because they don't fit into the expectations of society.

When a person learns to lie to escape punishment, ridicule, and judgment and create a false persona to fit into the world, he or she immediately stops trusting him- or herself and all others who do the same. Even worse, people get so used to the created persona that, usually on a conscious level, the true self is forgotten. Subconsciously and superconsciously, there is a part of everyone that knows the truth in every situation, which usually doesn't match what is being portrayed. We *all* know when a person is lying or when a situation is not beneficial to our well-being, but we often override that knowledge and rationalize it by focusing on some aspect of the person or situation that we find is of value to us at the time. When the lies are disclosed or the situation turns out to be unhealthy, we say we can't trust others, which deepens the subconscious belief in this statement as well. It is important to accept that the other person/self and all of your external experience are mirrored reflections of *you* and your hidden lies. Your true self wants very much for you to identify the false persona you have created and to consciously choose to let it go.

Trust issues are fear based, from the fear of being lied to; fear of others knowing we are lying; fear of not being loved or lovable; fear of others knowing the truth (judgment of self/false belief) that we are bad people; fear of others not following through with what they said or promised; fear of things not turning out the way we want; fear that we are incompetent, fear we are not in control of our own lives, others' lives, and the world we live in; and on the deepest level, fear that there really is no God/life force/Source/higher power that has our back and exists with/as us. This boils down to the fear that we are in this all alone. This is truly the foundation of all fear and trust issues.

Trust issues, just as everything you experience, is *all about you* and your relationship with yourself, other selves, and Source/life. Because of this, the way to resolve trust issues is not about how trustworthy another is, it's how trustworthy you are and how much you choose to trust in your intimate relationship with Source as Source. Trust that you are one with the infinite intelligence that is flowing through you, as you, guiding you through all your experiences. The ultimate resolution to all trust issues, which your Source self is asking of you, is to completely let go of all resistance, choosing to trust and flow with the current of life while it is purifying you into the highest vibrational version of you. As the well-known childhood rhyme says, "Row, Row, Row your boat, gently down the stream, merrily, merrily, merrily, life is but a dream.

Chapter 9.
Authentic Self

**"We are constantly invited to be
who we are."
— Henry David Thoreau**

We all have a yearning to be our authentic selves and express our genuine thoughts, feelings, and actions freely without the fear of judgment, punishment, and alienation. One of the basic reasons for the union of two people in an intimate relationship is to provide a safe haven for each to be themselves. But unfortunately, even in many marriages and intimate partnerships, people still don't feel safe enough to reveal *all* of them. I have heard many stories from couples who, even after 40 years of marriage, are still hiding parts of themselves from the other. It can be frightening for ourselves and others when the not-so-pretty dark side reveals itself.

Most people don't realize the detrimental impact a lifetime of suppressed thoughts and emotions has on them, their loved ones, and the world we all share. The collection of these neglected thoughts and emotions create what is often called the Shadow Self.

We all have a Shadow Self – it's the aspect of you that has been judged as bad or unacceptable and is usually buried deep in the subconscious mind. It's a very powerful thought form that is created from mostly fear-based emotions like anger, resentment, shame, and jealousy, but also very common are sexual thoughts that are believed to be wrong or deviant. In this context, a powerful thought form is one that has a tremendous amount of influence on your thoughts, actions, and reactions throughout your daily life. As you continue to suppress emotions, it grows in strength, and the more powerful it gets, the harder it becomes to hide. This causes the drama, hostility, violence, and trauma in people's lives and society as a whole. It's the cause of most of the mass shootings and violent acts against others and the self. The tendency is to project the Shadow Self onto others, and the projection of a nation's Collective Shadow onto another nation. This is when we displace the blame of the internal shadow out onto others. The Shadow Self is prevalent in all humans, and the rulers of nations use strategic methods of propaganda to fuel this aspect of humanity to utilize their control over them. They use national superiority, anger, fear, hatred, and separatism. We are all aware of the immense power Hitler acquired using these tactics, we also need to realize that it's still being used by almost all of the world rulers. But again, it's not just the rulers who do this; we all do it in our lives to some degree.

We are all one within the collective consciousness of humanity, which represents the *full spectrum* of thoughts, emotions, actions, and memories. That includes all of the most horrific and greatest moments in human experience. *Everyone is the potential of the entire spectrum*, and it can be terrifying when we see the Shadow Self in others and even more so when we recognize it in ourselves. It takes courage to own up to all that we are, and the time is **now** to be courageous and claim back our innate power that has been wasted, hiding aspects of ourselves.

We need to create a loving and accepting space for ourselves and others to process and integrate a healthier version of the Shadow Self. It will take time and lots of love, but when more of us choose to do the work needed for this transformation, then we will naturally and vibrationally give permission for others to do the same. *Everyone* is dealing not only with his or her individual Shadow Self, but also with the collective shadow of humanity. We are all in the midst of a rapid transformation collectively, and there are at our disposal hundreds of books, trainings, therapies, videos, and programs to help understand, transform, and integrate the Shadow Self.

To be your authentic self is to accept and express all that you are and to live with the integrity of your own truth. As you do this, your Shadow Self will become a healthier and more integrated expression of you. Each being on this planet is responsible for doing their individual work towards evolving into the authentic expression of Source through/as them, knowing that, as they do this, they are contributing to the evolution of the collective. *This is why we are here… this is Source/your plan.* Ultimately, we will be free of all energies that inhibit us from being the pure expression of Source in human form.

Many people say that, after so many years of lying, hiding, and being what they are supposed to be, they have no idea who or what their authentic self is. My suggestion is to write down these four questions and meditate on them daily:

1. If you knew it didn't matter to anyone else what you do, what would you do?
2. If you knew you were going to succeed at whatever you did, what would you do?
3. If you knew you only had 6 months left to live, what would you do?
4. If you had 100 million dollars in the bank, what would you do?

Chapter 10:
Impersonal Life

**"In this universe, which was created by a divine
organizing intelligence,
there are simply no accidents."
– Wayne Dyer**

Look around in nature, the cosmos, and your own body. There is obviously an intelligent force creating, organizing, and orchestrating *everything*. How does an oak seed become a tree? How did the basic organisms evolve into animals and humans? How did the universe and our galaxy create the perfect atmosphere for human life? How did we form from the fertilization of the egg into a human body and maintain the balance of a perfectly functioning system? The answer is intelligence; universal consciousness, from the mind of Source. There is an implicate order and an innate balancing mechanism to all that was created and all that will manifest in the perceived physical reality. All that exists is interrelated and depends on everything else.

Planet Earth is an experiential field of universal consciousness that is an ever-evolving, balanced, holistic life force. It was created as an opportunity for Source to experience itself through all the constantly transforming, seemingly individual expressions of life – from the microbe to the human. Not one aspect is more important than another. *All* expressions are necessary and interdependent for the entirety of experience.

The law of polarity is used for balance and reflection. All perceived opposites co-exist; this illustrates the proverbial other side of the coin. Opposites give us a chance to experience both sides: light (love) and dark (fear). Each being has, is, and will experience both sides of the spectrum and all of the points in between. We *are* all of it. By experiencing the full spectrum, we accept and integrate all that we are. All judgment of self diminishes, and we become understanding, compassionate, forgiving, allowing, and loving, bringing us back to our essence, the pure expression of unconditional love and acceptance for *all that exists.*

That is the plan that Source/*we* all conceived. *Everyone* experiencing this timeline has the potential and opportunity for self-realization, remembrance of *what* we are and *why* we are here – to take human evolution for a quantum leap. The human species and the planet we share is in the process of an exponential transmutation, and *everyone/everything* is playing a role in this endeavor, from the saint to the most heinous criminal, and all of us in between. It may be difficult to grasp the idea that the saint and criminal can both play an important role in our evolution, but if you truly realize that we are all *one* as the Universal Field of Consciousness, evolving together as *one*, then you know that *everyone* is contributing and equally valuable. That horrible murderer can give someone the chance to choose to transform feelings of anger, hatred, judgment, and condemnation into understanding, forgiveness, and even compassion and unconditional love. I know this seems unthinkable, but it does happen, and when it does, what a HUGE experiential and transformative shift in consciousness it is for both the assailant and assailed. As Buddha said, "Hatred does not cease by hatred, but only by love. This is the eternal rule." There are very deep layers of meaning to events that most are not even close to being aware of.

The more you tune in to the intelligence of universal consciousness, you see how it works its brilliant wonders through each one of us and all that exist in every moment of existence. It communicates with us through our intuition, gut feeling, a deep knowing, dreams, and sychronicities. When you first start to tune in, you become aware of more synchronicities. Then, when your personal vibrational field not just tunes in but embodies the higher frequencies of universal intelligence, you realize that *everything happening is a synchronicity; nothing is personal.* It is all playing out as the already-created plan of Source/*you.*

Chapter 11.
Superhuman

"If ye have faith as a grain of mustard seed, ye shall say unto this mountain, Remove hence to yonder place; and it shall remove; and nothing shall be impossible unto you."
– Jesus

It's a hot topic: humans are in the midst of a mind/body/consciousness upgrade. We are morphing into the supramental version of human. This term came from Mother, the visionary of the most awesome community Auroville in India. Mother and her partner Guru Sri Aurobindo dedicated their lives to manifesting on earth a mode of human consciousness that was beyond the conscious and subconscious mind, which they called the supermind or the supramental. They imagined that this advance in human consciousness would transform humans into an entirely new species.

As shown in the national best-selling book, Stealing Fire, it is our innate nature to do anything we can to escape the limited conscious, subconscious, and collective consciousness and merge into the flow of the superconsciousness. Through raising the personal energetic vibrational field and lowering our brainwaves, humans flow unrestricted intelligence of universal consciousness and become superheros. They are able to mentally and physically perform to their greatest potential in the moment. This happens when athletes go beyond themselves and perform superhuman feats; artists allow the music, images, and words to flow through them to manifest masterpieces; scientists, inventors, and programmers receive their breakthrough ideas. There has always been a certain percentage of people who have utilized the state of flow either consciously or unconsciously, but what's happening now is a huge awakening within the human race to let go of the conditioned mind and flow as a superhuman self.

There's a reason that there are so many movies, TV shows, books, and comics about superheros or people with super powers. In the DC Comic universe, a metahuman is a human with superpowers. This archetype resonates with our true self. On a conscious level, most want to be like superheros and have superpowers. However, on the superconscious level, we *know* we are beyond human, we *have* the potential for super powers, we *are* superhuman.

Spiritual masters were known to have magical, supernatural, paranormal powers. The ancient texts note that they were able to bi-locate, walk through walls, walk on water, levitate, heal others, change the elements, and so forth. It is said that these superhuman abilities came from mastering their minds through meditation.

Thankfully for all of us, the new very powerful frequencies we are being bathed in from universal consciousness is provoking an awakening of people all over the world, causing a ripple effect within the collective consciousness and amplifying the unified transformation. This does not mean daily meditation is not important, but that it's not necessary for most to be isolated in a cave or monastery. The momentum of the collective is lessening the individual burden.

What *is* required from each of us is to continue with daily meditation, do the individual work with inquiry, heal the emotional body with Ho'oponopno, consciously invite and allow the new higher vibrational frequencies of universal consciousness to be integrated and embodied, and surrender as often as possible to the selfless, effortless, and timeless state of flow.

Chapter 12.
Imagination, Assumption, and Surrender

"Limitations live only in our minds.
But if we use our imaginations,
Our possibilities become limitless.
—Jamie Paolinetti

The only thing stopping you from becoming the ideal you and experiencing all that your heart and soul desire is the current concept of you and the world you live in, based on the data you have in your subconscious mind. As you perform the practices already given in the previous chapters, the next step is using the immense power of imagination, assumption, and surrender. There is no limit to imagination combined with the assumption that your desire is already created and with 100% surrender to the way it unfolds.

Mystics and consciousness teachers such as Eckart Tolle as well as physicists say that time is an illusion:

"The dividing line between past, present, and future is an illusion." – Albert Einstein

There is in fact no division of time. Everything that has ever existed or ever will exist, exists *now*. What your senses perceive are really just a series of snapshots of moments, just a momentary slice of all existence in space-time, popping in and out of your reality. Your own perception of what is happening is filtered though your biological system, senses, brain, and data in the subconscious mind. All that ever existed and ever will exist already does so within the infinite dimensions of creation.

Knowing this, we realize we cannot actually create anything, because it has already been created. What we can do is use our focused imagination to align our vibrational frequency with the ideal of who we want to be, what we want to experience, and what we want to have. If you have a true desire for something, then it surely is already created, waiting and wanting to be materialized and experienced. It is wanting to experience through you as much as you want to experience it, so just *be* it. All of the infinite possibilities that exist in the non-physical dimensions are a thought of creation waiting to be manifested. All you have to do is align with it. As Paulo Coelho said, "If we seek something, that same thing is seeking us."

The first step in using imagination to change the concept of yourself and start manifesting your dream life is *desire*. You must be clear within your heart and mind as to what you desire; you must want it with all of your being. Use the practice of imagination while you are in a relaxed state of mind. The best times are when you are just starting to fall asleep, or when you just wake up and are still partially in the sleep state, or during meditation. Imagination and attention work hand in hand. It's important to keep your attention on the subjective within and disregard the objective without, in order to eliminate distractions. The subjective is that in which you make the desired changes and imagine the new you/life as experience. You add great energy to your desire with focused attention to it. From the moment you begin using imagination to change your life, it is imperative that you have focused attention on only that which you desire and not permit anything contrary to that in your field of attention. *Everything* that manifests from the non-physical dimensions is through the energy of thought/imagination.

The second step is assuming without a doubt that your desire has already been created and it's just waiting for you to align with it. The power of assumption comes by becoming it, not just thinking about it. You have to become consumed by it with every part of you. You bring the imagined state into your daily life and become the guardian of any thoughts, emotions, words, or deeds that do not resonate with it. If you notice a behavior that doesn't resonate, you immediately use the bubble technique to release it from your consciousness. You become committed and persistent in the vision, imagination, and energy of the ideal. You visualize it from its end point, as though you already are and have it. Using all the senses in your imagination and *feeling* what it feels like to be it, feel the ecstasy of joy, smell the beauty of your surroundings, hear the song of your words, and see how others react to you and your environment as the ideal who embodies all that you desire. Be, feel, and express deep gratitude for being your desire as IF you already have it.

The final and most important step is *surrender.* Unite your being with your desire, and completely surrender to it with such awareness of its reality that you lose your old concept of self and life and enter the new. Now, with complete trust and faith in your relationship with life, you allow the most beneficial reality to manifest that which is aligned with Source/your plan. Through surrender, you may not experience exactly what your conscious mind conjures up, but it will be aligned with your superconscious mind and the highest good for your personal and the collective development.

When one surrenders 100% to the superconscious, they align their mind/soul/body with the original plan for incarnation. He or she listens to the messages from Source coming from all the various daily encounters, follow the flow of life, and revel in the constant miraculous beauty of the infinite mind unfolding through the evolution of life on Earth.

Chapter 13.
Meditation

"Meditation is the dissolution of thoughts in eternal awareness or pure consciousness without objectification, knowing without thinking, merging finitude in infinity."
– Voltaire

Throughout my years as a Transformation Facilitator, people have asked, "If you could only give one piece of advice, what would it be?" My answer is always, "Meditate daily!" Make it as important as drinking water, eating, and sleeping; include it in your daily life as though you cannot live without it. Set a time like you would a meeting, and make it clear in your mind that this is a meeting you cannot miss. The meeting with *you* as Source.

When you meditate daily, you will gradually start to notice that you are bringing that deep connection and serene state of being you feel with you throughout the course of your day. People will feel very comfortable with you and will naturally tune in to your calming vibration, and like a tuning fork, they will resonate with you.

Meditation assists in cleansing the mind/body of all that is not true. It holds space for the limiting data of the subconscious mind and deep suppressed emotions in the body to come to the surface so that you can *thank* them, *love* them, and *release* them to the universe to be transmuted. It is very powerful if you use Ho'oponopono when these emotions arise.

As you start to meditate daily, your entire way of perceiving yourself, others, and the world will change. Your awareness will expand into the multidimensional layers of existence, allowing you see and sense clearly past the illusion of physical reality and into the consciousness of infinite possibilities.

Famous athletes, actors, musicians, novelists, artists, and leaders of business and politics use meditation to enhance their work and daily lives. There are a over a hundred physical, mental, emotional, and spiritual benefits from meditation, and many have been proven scientifically. The ultimate benefit is **remembering that there is only one relationship – Source with Source as you.** Lose yourself in the *I am* awareness of that fact.

Meditation cleanses the mental, emotional, physical, spiritual, and energetic body from false limiting data that affects humans on all levels of experience, while providing the aspects of your true, pure, empowered self to emerge. Just as there are many benefits, there are also many ways of meditating, all of which lead you to the same place: the **real you**!

I grew up in a family of metaphysicians, so I was taught as a child how to enter "the silence" for mediation from my grandfather, who founded the Institute of Cosmic Wisdom. When I was young, I enjoyed lying in the grass and merging myself into the earth, and as a teenager in Hawaii, I spent hours each day lying on the beach, dissolving my entire being into the sun. At the time, I didn't realize this was also meditation. Meditation is anything that removes you from the conscious thinking mind and leaves you with just awareness; being connected to the essence of you, in the flow, with no thought. Athletes, musicians, artists, inventors, yoga practitioners, or anyone who experiences very focused attention on one thing naturally loses conscious thought and enters into the meditative state of flow.

I have learned and taught various methods of meditation through all the different phases of my life, and my personal recommendation is to use the meditation in Chapter 1 along with an additional layer. After you have raised your energetic vibration and dissolved all of your being into it, then just be *aware* of the presence of source. If thoughts come into mind, bring yourself back to the feeling of your energy body and then back to awareness. If deep emotions come up, then use Ho'oponopono on them. If this one doesn't work well enough for you, then just place your intention out into the universe that you would like the best meditation style for you at this stage in your life. The universe is sure to respond, and it will be revealed to you very soon.

Chapter 14:
Love

**"Love is not an emotion,
it's your very existence."
— Rumi**

Love is the purest frequency of the universal field of consciousness, the essence of all that exists. It is *your essence*. It's the nectar of life. When we think we love someone or something, we feel a connection, and at the superconscious level of mind, we recognize the oneness of this essence in them and ourselves.

Unfortunately, the false data of what love is that's programmed into our subconscious from the collective consciousness as well as our past experiences affects what we believe and how we behave towards giving and receiving love.

The most delicious and natural feeling of recognizing your true self in someone or something has been tainted by the conditioned human mind. The mind conceives love as affection, desire, wanting, need, and attachment. We base our love on our ever-fluctuating emotions. Experiencing love as an emotion tunes us into the law of polarity's swing between emotional love's opposite, which is fear. The phrase "falling in love" is so perfect, because the moment your subconscious computes the high feeling of love as an emotion, it then immediately offers the opposite, the falling down into fear. As soon as you feel the fear of loss, then you automatically go into control and attachment.

I was gifted with a life experience that saved me from the up and down rollercoaster ride of falling in and out of love. I had been addicted to the high of romantic love since my early teens. I loved romantic movies, music, and anything that had to do with romance – I believed romance was love. My family environment was very dysfunctional, so not only did I have an unhealthy example of love as a child, but I also used the idea of romantic love to rescue me from the darkness of my life. Through many years of experiencing the pain of the fall, I became focused on finding out what love really is. I told the universe, "I want the ultimate love relationship!" I decided to do research and write a book called <u>What Is Love?</u> (one I didn't finish). As I was diving deep into the research, I fell in love. It was different this time; it was what I imagined to be the ultimate love relationship, one with a soulmate. There were no expectations or attachments; we had total trust and a deep connection mentally, emotionally, physically, and spiritually. I thought I had finally done it; I had broken free form my pattern and found true love. I was not flying on the clouds, I was way above them. Then the phone call came: he was breaking up with me. As he was telling me why, I began to feel the fall. With tears streaming down my face, I screamed in my mind to the Universe: *Why?? What's wrong with me, why can't I keep this ultimate love?* In that moment, I got the answer. I realized I didn't have to fall, but that the high of love was *mine*. I realized I *allowed* myself to *be* love more than I ever have, and it wasn't about him, it was *all about me*. He was just a reflection of the love that *I am*, that I allowed to flow through and be expressed as me. I chose from that moment to stay high in love, to never fall out again. It is mine! I *am* love. Before I had entered that relationship, I made it clear to the universe that I wanted to experience the ultimate love relationship, which I thought at the time was a soulmate union. The universe gave me what I asked for, but it wasn't what I thought; it was way more. It was *me* with *me*, as Source. Through this experience, I learned that love is *not* about desiring someone, wanting to be with them, a need to have them in your life, exchanging affection, or finding your soulmate. Rather, love is what you and I are! It is the vibrational essence of all existence. It is impossible to be without love, and there is absolutely no reason to want or need love because love is what we are. Love is meant to be expressed, shared, and experienced. It is our most basic nature to love and be loved. There is no limit to how much you can love, because you and the entire universe are infinitely endowed as love. You are experiencing the most intimate relationship with love as love, and most of you do not remember this. When you remember yourself as love, then you recognize all other selves as love and become in love with all of life.

Being in love is a great high, the ultimate human experience. It has the power to heal even the most wounded people. When you are experiencing this consciousness of love and in a personal relationship, you know you are a reflection of each other and hold a nonjudgmental, unconditional loving space, as each one is doing the inner work for the purification of mind, body, and soul. You know that this is the sole and soul reason you are together. In a conscious relationship, both work together to help each other cleanse from the subconscious mind all of the fear-based ideas, concepts, and beliefs that are restricting them from being the pure and free expression of Source, as them. They take full responsibility for their own thoughts and feelings and do the work to cleanse the ones that are not in alignment with their true self. They release all feelings of need, attachment, expectations, and control over the other and instead allow acceptance and love to prevail. They are aware that their union is perfectly orchestrated by their superconscious for self-realization. This is the true purpose for all relationships. Clear the way to remember and know that there is really only one relationship – **Source with Source as you.**

Chapter 15.
Relationship

"The universe is saying: allow me to flow through you unrestricted, and you will see the greatest magic you have ever seen."
– Klaus Joehle

If you have been practicing the mediation in Chapter 1, then you have acquainted yourself with your energy/light field and realize it is your individual energy-signature within universal consciousness. You know or are becoming aware that you are in an intimate relationship, constantly communicating and transferring energy and information to everyone and everything. When you exchange energy with others, you are giving and receiving energetic life force with them.

The seeming physical reality is 99.99% energy/light, and everything you do and interact with uses and exchanges energy – thinking, talking, eating, breathing, digesting, everything – energy is the currency of the universe.

When an infant is in the womb, its energy field is one with its mother's energy field. This new symbiotic relationship with the mother is the beginning of confusion and loss of memory of being one with the energetic universal field of consciousness. When the infant is born and the umbilical cord is cut, not only does the process bring the shock of being disconnected from the mother, but it also ignites the most primal fear of separation from both mother and the infinite supply of energetic life force of universal consciousness.

Cuddling, caressing, and sharing love with a newborn infant are acts of paying attention and giving them life-force energy. The forgetting process strengthens as they begin to rely on others for their source of energetic life force, love, and power. Children grow up craving attention and energy to feel safe and fulfilled. When there are multiple children in a family, it is very common to compete with each other over the attention or energy of a caregiver. They will then devise their own strategic ability within the newly forming ego to get attention. Some children become the problem child (negative attention is still energy!), and some children will be the perfect child. There are various clever ways a child will conceive of to get attention. The more attention one gets, the more empowered and safe he or she feels.

Childhood is the beginning of a lifetime quest for the continuous supply of energetic life force from someone or something outside of oneself. We supplement it with the idea that love from another will sustain us. If we lose the other, we feel we have lost love and our source of life force energy. Often when a guardian or life partner dies, a person believes he or she cannot survive without that loved one. We have forgotten that *we are* the infinite field of universal consciousness and love. Forgetting this, we have this deep sense of need for others, and many learn to manipulate, control, and disempower others in order to obtain their life energy and feel more empowered and safe.

We soon start utilizing other sources of energy exchange for the false feeling of nourishment, empowerment, and safety, such as through money, social recognition, acceptance, and all other forms of achievement people strive for. If you look around with pure awareness, you will see that *every* action, exchange, and interaction in the perceived physical reality is an exchange of energy and information. *Everything is energy!*

Being aware of this fact allows you to clearly see how you relate to, and the quality of your relationship with, everyone and everything. Do you believe that if you are in a supportive romantic relationship, feel loved by others, are accepted, and recognized socially or have more money and power, then your life will be good and you will be happier? This is the common false belief in the human collective conscious that entraps all of us into the insatiable egoic pursuit for something outside ourselves to give us a feeling of happiness, fulfillment, and safety. We have forgotten that *we are* fully empowered and pure unconditional love, with access to an infinite supply of energy within the field of universal consciousness. Until we realize this truth, we will always feel deeply that something is missing, incomplete, or unfulfilled, no matter how much money, attention, recognition, acceptance, power, and love from others we get. A good example of this is to look at how many famous people who are extremely wealthy, socially popular, loved, recognized, and accepted develop addiction to alcohol, drugs, and sex. They go in and out of rehab, die from overdose, get depressed, and remain unhappy while grasping for more money, fame, and false power.

The *most important* step for transformation in human evolution and true fulfillment, sovereignty, and joy in life is to realize/remember that everything that exists, including you, is Source in a relationship with itself as you, and all of the infinite expressions of the universal field of consciousness. This is *the one only relationship* that truly exists. If you turn your focus onto that relationship and recognize it as the most important and *only* relationship there is, you fortify yourself in that relationship and allow the universal life force energy to flow through you uninhibited, with total trust and complete surrender, and then you will become the fully empowered and truly enriched expression of Source.

Chapter 16:
ONENESS

All of existence is in the most intimate relationship with itself as the unified infinite expressions of The One – Source. There is only one relationship to experience, and that is Source with Source as *you* and all that exists. You will remember this naturally when you awaken from the amnesia of the collective consciousness. You become aware of the connection and relationship with everything around you. You can see, sense, and feel your energetic waves of information interacting and influencing everything and everyone as their waves impact you. When you tune into and align with the awakened state of consciousness, you know without a doubt that *you are everything, and everything is you.*

The following quotes come from some of the most influential people around the world who have awakened to the consciousness of oneness and seek to share their views with you:

"The physical universe was created when Oneness became duality, and we can see this duality, this yin and yang everywhere in the universe; in every atom, every action, and every function of the human body. Yin and yang are manifest everywhere except at the very center of being, the perfect point of balance at infinite moment of now where the future becomes the past. This overcoming of all the usual barriers between the individual and the Absolute is the great mystic achievement. In mystic states, we both become one with the Absolute and become aware of our oneness. This is the everlasting and triumphant mystical tradition hardly altered by difference of crime or creed."
– William James

"A group of largely unknown frontier scientific explorers suggests that, at our essence, we exist as a unity, a relationship – utterly interdependent, the parts
affecting the whole."
– Lynn Mctaggart

"For there is one universe made up of all things, and one god who pervades all things, and one substance, and one law,
and one reason"
- Marcus Aurelius

"I believe that Jesus realized his oneness with God,
and what he attempted to do was show the way to all
of us, how to realize our own oneness with God
also, so he's a precursor."
– Eckhart Tolle

"There is one mind common to all individual men.
Every man is an inlet to the same and to all of the
same. He that is once admitted to the right of reason
is made a free man of the whole estate. What Plato
has thought, he may think; what a saint has felt, he
may feel; what at any time has befallen any man, he
can understand. Who hath access to this universal
mind is a party to all that is or can be done, for this
is the only and sovereign agent."
– Ralph Waldo Emerson

"We each have a sixth sense that is attuned to the
oneness dimension in life, providing a means for us
to guide our lives in accord
with our ideas."
– Henry Reed

"When we view ourselves in space and time, our
consciousnesses are obviously the separate
individuals of a particle-picture, but when we pass
beyond space and time, they may perhaps form
ingredients of a single continuous stream of life. As
it is with light and electricity, so it may be with life;

the phenomena may be individuals carrying on
separate existences in space time, while in the deeper
reality beyond space and time we may be all
members of one body."
– Sir James Jeans, Astrophysicist

"A person experiences life as something separated
from the rest, a kind of optical delusion of
consciousness. Our task must be to free ourselves
from this selfimposed prison, and through
compassion, to find the reality of oneness."
– Albert Einstein

"The glory which You have given Me I have given to
them, that they may be one,
just as We are one."
– Jesus

"At the deepest level, an open heart is a spacious
presence, in which the sense of separation between
yourself and the other dissolves, and there is the
recognition of oneness, of shared consciousness.
That recognition is love. Sensing the formless
essence in another and recognizing it as one with
your own essence – that's what love is. All this is an
intrinsic part of the awakened consciousness and the
revelation of the spiritual dimension of life."
– Eckhart Tolle

"You can develop the right attitude toward others if
you have kindness, love, and respect for them, and a
clear realization of the oneness of all human beings."
– Dalai Lama

"The first peace, which is the most important, is that
which comes within the souls of people when they
realize their relationship, their oneness with the
universe and all it's powers, and when they realize at
the center of the universe dwells the great spirit, and
that this center is really everywhere, it is
within each one of us."
– Black Elk

"To divide or multiply consciousness is something
meaningless. In all the world, there is no kind of
framework within which we can find consciousness
in the plural; this is simply something we construct
because of the spatio-temporal plurality of
individuals, but it is a false construction. The
category of number, of whole and parts, are then
simply not applicable to it…. The overall number of
minds is just one… In truth
there is only one mind."
– Erwin Schrodinger,
1933, Nobel Prize in Physics

"The essence of spirituality is to be constantly aware
of the oneness of all, at the same time to celebrate
the uniqueness of the individual."
– Jaggi Vasudey

"We must realize that it is best to focus on our
oneness to re-emphasize what is the same about
each of us rather than dwell
on what is different."
– Dalai Lama

"I believe in absolute oneness of God
and therefore also humanity."
– Mahatma Gandhi

"The heart of the matter is always our oneness with
divine spirit,
our union with all life."
– Nhat Hanh

"Those who are highly evolved maintain an
undiscriminating perception. Seeing everything,
labeling nothing, they maintain their awareness of
the Great Oneness. Thus, they are supported by it."
– Laozi

"Love is the recognition of oneness
in the world of duality."
– Eckhart Tolle

"I share the belief of many of my contemporaries
that the spiritual crises pervading all spheres of
Western industrial society can be remedied only by a
change in our world view. We shall have to shift
from the materialistic, dualistic belief that people and
their environment are separate, toward a new
consciousness of an all-encompassing reality, which
embraces the experiencing ego, a reality in which
people feel their oneness with animate nature and all
of creation."
– Albert Hofmann

"We all drink from one water. We all breathe from
one air. We rise from one ocean.
And we live under one sky."
– Anwar Fazal

"God is unity, but always works in variety."
– Ralph Waldo Emerson

"All differences in this world are of degree, and not
of kind, because oneness is the secret of everything."
– Swami Vivekananda

"Love is how it feels to recognize our essential unity.
Awakening to oneness is the experience of Big Love.
Knowing you are one with all,
you find yourself in love with all."
– Timothy Freke

"From out of all the many particulars comes
oneness, and out of oneness comes
all the many particulars."
– Heraclitus

"But I'll tell you what hermits realize, if you go off
into a far, far forest and get very quiet, you'll come
to understand that you're connected with
everything."
– Alan Watts

"He who experiences the unity of life sees his own
self in all beings and all beings
in his own self."
– Buddha

"But can anyone doubt today that all the millions of
individuals and all the innumerable types and
characters constitute an entity, a unit? Though free
to think and act, we are held together, like the stars
in the firmament, with ties inseparable."
– Nikola Tesla

"I saw my Lord with the Eye of my heart, and I said:
Truly there is no doubt that it is you. It is You that I
see in everything. And I do not see You through
anything (but you)."
– Al-Hallam

There is one mind common to all individual men…
[a] universal mind. The Over-Soul is that unity…
within which every man's particular being is
contained and made one with all other. Within man
is the soul of the whole… the eternal *one*."
– Ralph Waldo Emerson

"All things are implicated with one another, and the
bond is holy, and there is hardly anything
unconnected with any other things. For things have
been coordinated, and they combine to make up the
same universe. For there is one universe made up of
all things, and one God who pervades all things, and
one substance, and one law, and one reason." –
Marcus Aurelius

"There is one common flow, one common
breathing, all things are in sympathy."
— Hippocrates

"In the stillness of your presence, you can feel your
own formless and timeless reality as the
unmanifested life that animates your physical form.
You can then feel the same life deep within every
other human and every other creature. You look
beyond the veil of form and separation. This is the
realization of oneness. This is love."
– Eckhart Tolle

"Each time a man looks into your eyes, he is only
searching to find himself, for he knows already that
he is part of you."
– Jeremy Aldana

"Each person you meet is an aspect of yourself,
clamoring for love."
– Eric Micha'el Lev

"Most of the world's religions serve only to
strengthen attachments to false concepts such as self
and other, life and death, heaven and earth, and so
on. Those who become entangled in these false ideas
are prevented from perceiving
the Integral Oneness."
– Laozi

"It's difficult to believe in yourself, because the idea
of self is an artificial construction. You are in fact
part of the glorious oneness of the universe.
Everything beautiful in the world is within you."
– Russell Brand

"As soon as a man stands up and says he is right or
his church is right and all others are wrong, he is
himself all wrong. He does not know that upon the
proof of all the others depends on the proof of his
own. Love and charity for the whole human race –
that is the test of true religiousness. I do not mean

the sentimental statement that all men are brothers,
but that one must feel the oneness of human life."
– Swami Vivekananda

"People normally cut reality into compartments and
so are unable to see the interdependence of all
phenomena. To see one in all and all in one is to
break through the great barrier which narrows one's
perception of reality."
– Nhat Hanh

"Through our eyes, the universe perceives itself.
Through our ears, the universe is listening to its
harmonies. We are the witnesses through which the
universe becomes conscious of its glory,
of its magnificence."
– Alan Watts

"Learn how to see. Realize everything connects to
everything else."
–Leonardo da Vinci

"Find the good. Seek the unity.
Ignore the divisions among us."
– Aristotle

"View all religions as a part of a single system – one
unified and continuous series of divinely-inspired

teachers who all revealed the spiritual and mystical
knowledge humanity needed
at the time they appeared."
– Baha'i teaching

"Only humility will lead us to unity
and unity will lead us to peace."
– Mother Teresa

"I have long held an opinion, almost amounting to
conviction, in common I believe with many other
lovers of natural knowledge, that the various forms
under which the forces of matter are made manifest
have one common origin; or, in other words, are so
directly related and mutually dependent, that they are
convertible, as it were, one into another,
and possess equivalents
of power in their action."
– Michael Faraday

"Each one of us has an essential role in
the whole of humanity."
– Oprah Winfrey

"A belief in separation is always at the root of a
problem, and a realization of our oneness is always
at the root of its solution."
– Marianne Williamson

"The notion of a separate organism is clearly an abstraction, as is also its boundary. Underlying all this is unbroken wholeness, even though our civilization has developed in such a way as to strongly emphasize the separation into parts."
– David Bohm and Basil Hiley, Physicist

"Human nature was originally one,
and we were a whole."
– Plato

About the Author

Cher was born into a family of metaphysicians. She learned as a child how to enter what her grandfather called "the silence", which she later learned was meditation. Due to this upbringing she did not lose the natural conscious connection to other dimensions beyond physical. She is known to be an empath with the uncanny ability to see the energetic blockages in a person, find the original trauma behind it, and assist the person in transmuting and releasing it in one session.

In her youth she personally experienced and observed in others much trauma and detrimental false conditioning. At 17 she started traveling the world looking for the newest and best way to help herself and others clear and transmute the limiting false beliefs, traumas, and energies that have been acquired through life experience and the collective consciousness of humanity. She became what she called "an Info junkie", meeting healers and spiritual teachers, attending hundreds of seminars with the leaders in Mind/Body Medicine, acquiring numerous certifications, completing internships, reading thousands of books, and clearing clients. She had a private practice as a Mind/Body/Spirit Therapist and Transformational Facilitator for over 30 years, owned a Yoga School, founded a Divorce Center for Women, and was the founder of a Re-programming Center for Women and Children.

In 2017 she started traveling the world again to help facilitate the evolution, expansion, and unification of human consciousness. She founded the project "Thank You for Being You" who's mission is to ignite the remembrance that all is One within the unified field of existence, and that everything/one is an unique expression and equally valuable part of the whole.

Her life mission is to help free humanity from all blocks so that we can unite consciously as our true selves, the one only self, Source, I *am*.

thankyouforbeingyou.love

www.ingramcontent.com/pod-product-compliance
Lightning Source LLC
Chambersburg PA
CBHW050647250726
48662CB00002B/538